The Ansonborough Boys

Charleston, SC
www.PalmettoPublishing.com

The Ansonborough Boys
Copyright © 2023 by Chester Sansbury

First Edition

Hardcover ISBN: 979-8-8229-0995-3
Paperback ISBN: 979-8-8229-0996-0

The Ansonborough Boys

By Chester Sansbury

Anson Street from the corner of
Society Street

Prologue

A Little History of Ansonborough

One of Charleston's least-remembered eigh-teenth-century neighborhoods was a suburban plantation known as "The Point," then "Rhett's Point" or "Rhettsbury," and later, "Trott's Point." This tract, which encompassed approximately thirty-five acres between King Street and the Cooper River, was as-sembled in the 1690s by Jonathan Amory, expanded in 1714 by William Rhett, and subdivided in 1773 by the husbands of Rhett's great-granddaughters. Most people today think of this property as comprising the southernmost part of the neighborhood called Ansonborough, but it has a history and identity of its own that deserves to be remembered. "Episode 53: Rhettsbury" *Charleston Time Machine*

George Street, which runs from Meeting to East Bay, was *not named* for King George. The honors go to Captain George Anson, the celebrated British naval officer (and privateer) who was stationed in Charles Town from 1724 to 1735 and for whom the Ansonborough area is named. When Ansonborough was developed as a suburb, five streets were laid out, each named to honor Captain Anson. George and Anson Streets honored the man himself. Three others were named for ships he commanded, i.e., Squirrel (now a part of Meeting Street), Scarborough (now part of Anson Street), and Centurion (now Society Street). Interestingly enough, Society Street was not named to reflect Charleston's well-known high society but rather for a school for orphan boys erected there by the venerable South Carolina Society in the mid-1700s. A portion of Wentworth Street also intersects Ansonborough and was named to honor Charles Watson Wentworth, Marquis of Rockingham, who actively supported the American cause prior to the Revolution (from *Charleston Living Magazine* May-June 2017).

The area had several houses occupied by slaves to serve the rich folk in other areas of Charleston, probably those below Broad Street. Such slave tenements evidently also extended north of Calhoun Street. After the Civil War, poor descendants of slaves still lived in the area including in dirt alleyways, two of which ran off Anson Street: one near 72 Anson and another near property now occupied by the Guillard auditorium.

In the early nineteenth century, as Charleston's new Centre Market in Market Street grew into a vibrant institution, all of the land between the market and Boundary (Calhoun) Street east of King Street became homogenized under the denomination of Ansonborough. Consider, if you will, the great Ansonborough fire of April 1838 that burned a large swath of land from East Bay to King Street, just north of the market. Nearly all of the real estate consumed in that terrible conflagration was actually once the property of Jonathan Amory, who trusted the Rhetts to protect it for his heirs. Three centuries after the demise of Mr. Amory and Colonel Rhett and all of their heirs, few who live in this neighborhood today remember the legacy of "The Point," or Rhettsbury. The next time you're strolling down Hasell Street, I recommend pausing in front of the old Rhett mansion at No. 54 to reimagine the scene. Though crowded and bustling today, that site was once a sort of genteel oasis lodged in a picturesque garden facing the morning sun rising over the Cooper River.

A saltwater creek known as Daniel Creek existed where Market Street and the market now exist.

Bodies of water used to ebb and flow in places we might not expect. A pond at the lower end of Meeting Street was filled by 1769. Vanderhorst Creek, which is now Water Street, was filled by 1792. The City Market and Market Street were built upon Governor's Creek between 1804 and 1807. By 1819 there was still much to be done to fill low lots and creek beds in what is now Harleston Village, including a creek between Beaufain and Wentworth streets.

Some of these creeks were scenic and popular. Cannon's Creek, which extended from the Ashley River toward Felix Street between Calhoun and Cannon Streets, was crossed by a bridge. According to a tour guide published in 1870, "Cannonsborough Bridge [as late as 1845] was a favorite resort in summer…but the gradual closing up of the land around it, and the continued increase of vehicles to and fro, have rendered it less agreeable…" (From *Charleston City Paper* by Evan R. Thompson, Aug. 21, 2013).

The Ansonborough fires of the early 1830s burned the mostly wooden houses that were common then. New structures were afterward built of brick. For example, the plaque on the house at 63 Anson states that it was built in 1838. Constructed ca. 1839 and rehabilitated in the late fifties to early sixties, it was one of two small gable-ended, masonry buildings (63 and 65 Anson Street) constructed as dependencies for 48 Society Street. Mrs. Robinson rented these properties separately before the Civil War. 63 Anson Street is listed as having been occupied by slaves in the 1861 census.

The Little Boys' Adventures

Preface

Things are not what they used to be. Little boys roamed freely while little girls stayed home. Who ever heard of wall walking, going barefoot to school, playing marbles for keeps in the dirt in school yards, coin fishing on King Street, fishing with Sunbeam bread balls in Colonial Lake, floating in the river on patched inner tube rafts, climbing on rooftops, riding on the top of slow moving rail cars, selling scrap metal at the junkyard, selling boiled peanuts (that Yankees never heard of) from a basket on King Street (while barefoot), eating squirrels, climbing Japanese plum trees seeking out the most juicy plums at the top and getting caught by a mean old biddy who threatened to call the police, selling sachets house to house for your drawers, searching for canned goods in railroad cars after the waterfront fire, looking for gold pieces of eight in a torn down house on Calhoun Street, seeing ghosts, getting stuck in pluff mud, delivering newspapers on a bike and rolling and slinging them to high porches, and many other adventures not heard of today.

We live life within and without ourselves. Our lives we can share with others, perhaps to inspire or entertain them. Whatever the reason, stories of life have meaning. They awaken our souls, and those of others too, to share their experiences and memories in hopes it may give meaning to our lives. So mote it be.

Come along and learn and enjoy a little of the past lives of little boys who lived in a slum area of Charleston in the late forties and early fifties that was once owned by a British lord and buccaneer.

LIFE IS AN ADVENTURE WE ALL ARE ON.
WE CHOOSE HOW TO LIVE IT UNTIL WE ARE GONE.

The Spirit of Ansonborough

One might ask if a city could have a personality, spirit, or a presence you could feel. Certainly for Charleston, it's the entire description. Growing up there, a sense of safety and a feeling that the city was a friend surrounding us allowed two brothers the freedom to make it theirs. Felt, but not thought about, it was like the old streets were our home. We didn't think about being safe or afraid of the people we passed, just smiling and exploring, and having fun and adventures.

Those quiet streets, each different, some wider, some curved, seemed to have that sense to look after two young boys who treated them as their own personal playground. The streets that have so much history that for over 250 years people walked down its same streets and sidewalks. The windows of the houses, with painted Charleston green shutters, close to the street open to several centuries of history passing by them; still there, after all this time. Changed, yes, but original bones still in all of them. Those houses must have absorbed some of those goings-on because they weren't changed much in the late forties and early fifties.

If you are from downtown Charleston, you can go home to the neighborhood where you grew up and many of them still look much like they did years ago. Sure, they have new paint, repairs, renovations, restorations, and a complete cast of new dwellers; many northerners or others from away inhabit the old homes. But it even feels much the same to little boys who grew up there. The narrow sidewalks still get too hot to walk on barefoot; you can walk across the streets wherever you want, and some of the older trees are still there. One can't help but think of the history that surrounds you on those hushed streets. Not "south of Broad," but the regal personality of the city still lingers there. Even a sense of pirates and ghosts who once could be seen can still be felt there.

A visitor wouldn't know that not too long ago the Ansonborough part of Charleston was a mixed neighborhood bordered by Meeting, Calhoun, East Bay, and Hasell Streets. Some once called it a slum. Blacks and whites intermeshed, living next door to each other. Families were friends with each other, regardless of color. They didn't lock their doors at night and shared many things. All in the past when this part of Charleston was a noble place of people trying to make a living and take care of their children, a few who were born at home without a doctor present, and sharing values, raising families, going to church, and wishing and working hard for a better life for themselves and their children.

The spirit is mostly still there among the locals, not noticed by the tourists. They visit and marvel at the real preserved historical beauty on each street and the restored stately houses and the few dilapidated-looking ones needing some care. Oh, if history could talk, what a marvelous story it could tell of this little community shining in a real American city, captured as a time capsule to be shared by those who walk those narrow sidewalks. They miss the spirit and the many lives that lived there in the past who called this place home.

Two young boys now in their senior years are still drawn back to a house on Anson Street, and to a city that was their friend when growing up. Those stories have become part of their family legacy and continue to live on. What a special gift to be shared from our "old friend," Ansonborough of Charleston. (written By Marshall, Chester's brother)

Along the Walk Home from School

It was really warm in my first grade class and hard not to sweat this day in early May. It was unpleasant during class this day because old Mrs. K, with her pulled-back gray hair with a tight knot and piercing eyes, had been mean to little Jimmy after cracking some other boy's knuckles with her always handy ruler. Quiet little Jimmy had raised his hand because he needed to pee really bad, but our old biddy of a seemly uncaring teacher wouldn't let him go to the bathroom just down the hall in this creaky old school with dark wooden floors on the corner of George and Saint Phillips Street. After a while I noticed little Jimmy was crying and then I saw the pee puddle under his chair. The gray-bunned, tall, and lanky old teacher then noticed it too and gruffly sent a little girl to get some help from the office. A nice younger woman came in and took Jimmy by the arm and they walked slowly out with Jimmy's head drooped amid the embarrassment dropped on this sad, meek, little boy. I guess they somehow got some dry pants for him, but he didn't come back that day. Luckily it was a Friday and things would likely be forgotten by Monday.

The bell rang to end the day and I was already thinking of what I could get to eat at home, because I'd only had a half pint of milk all day. I never had enough money to afford the regular school lunch but sometimes I was able to bring a nickel to buy some milk from the cafeteria and sometimes I brought a peanut butter and jelly sandwich on white bread from home with me. Occasionally, when I didn't have anything besides the milk, others who had plenty of food would share a sandwich with me. The loud bell rang and as I headed toward the door with the rush of the other kids, the gray-headed, mean master of the class shouted at me in her gruff voice everyone could hear, "you'd better get some shoes before you come back to class next time, Charlie!"

I headed quickly out through Bennett School's side, ground level entrance and across the dirt courtyard toward George Street. I went by other boys who were already starting to draw circles in the dirt to play marbles. First, they had to draw a line and throw a marble toward it to see who got closest to the line and would then shoot first at the marbles, clumped tightly together in the circle's middle. Every time you knocked a marble out of the circle and your bum stayed inside, you'd get another shot. The older sharpshooters sometimes cleaned the marbles out from the younger ones on their first turn. They played for keeps too, so you could really lose all your marbles. When I played, my favorite shooter was a slightly oversized clear blue crystal. I never got wiped out of my marbles.

Once on the street I was careful to stay on the shady side so my bare feet wouldn't get burned on the hot sidewalk, even though my soles were toughened. It was only about three blocks to home, but I was already thinking about what might be there to eat, perhaps a mayonnaise sandwich or peanut butter and sliced banana on white bread.

CORNER OF SOCIETY AND ANSON STREET.
ONE OF SEVERAL CORNER STORES IN OLD
ANSONBOROUGH.

THE ROYAL FOOD MARKET (78 ANSON STREET),
LOCATED AT THE NORTHEAST CORNER OF ANSON
STREET AND LAURENS STREET

Those Juicy Plums in Her Yard

That's about the time I passed a big old house on George Street, number 11, I believe, that had fading, chipped white paint on what looked like a three-story structure. I noticed a tall Japanese plum tree in the small front yard with two colored boys as high up as they could get on the limbs trying to grab the few remaining ripe, juicy looking orange plums. They gave up and scurried down from the tree and headed on down the street while I eyed those remaining ripe plums high up.

Those juicy yellow plums high up in the tree
were hard to resist,
So scampering up along the branches I went.
An old woman's beady black eyes
spied me from the window,
And she wasn't waiting to give me a kiss.
Then I knew it was too late to flee.

SHE GRABBED ME BY THE EAR,
AND INTO HER HOUSE I WENT
AND THERE TO DISAPPEAR.

As I scrambled up the tree a short way, I heard the front door of the house open and this dark haired, skinny old woman came out screaming something to me about breaking the limbs on her tree. She yelled at me to get down from there, and as I did, she grabbed me by one ear before I could run to the street. I squealed in pain, but she paid me no mind as I tried to tell her I didn't break those limbs and that those other boys did. But she continued to pull me, squirming, through the tall, wide front door into a dark, wide foyer with dark wooden floorboards. I eyed a big, closed door on the right side as she yanked me up some wide, steep, wooden stairs, around a landing, and onto the second floor, all the while ignoring my tears and yelling that she was going to call the police on me. She shoved me into a bathroom on the back side of the second floor and locked me in while I was suspecting she went to find a phone to call a policeman.

After a few minutes I looked around and noticed through the fairly large bathroom window, with a big wide frame, a pipe of some sort close by on the side of the house. I climbed up on the windowsill and fumbled with the latch and then I was able to slide it up enough to squeeze through and grab on to that pipe, gripping it with my bare toes as I slid quietly and swiftly to the ground, all the time eyeing a brick wall in the backyard as a possible escape route. I didn't waste any time running across the yard and pulling myself up onto the wall and carefully making my way along it like a cat to Meeting Street where I was able to move along the wide sidewalk unseen back to George Street where I ran as fast as I could down to Anson Street. I never looked back till I got home.

When I arrived, I slid in the single door on the side to our small, two-story, four-room house built in 1838 and once occupied by slaves and which perhaps had served as a tavern for pirates and a hangout for a few ghosts. Momma was busy as usual with the twin baby girls. She had a small frame, and her black hair was a mess today from the heat. Her dark, almost black, eyes looked tired. Twin two-year-old girls demanded a lot of her attention, and my older sister Julia was expected to help out with them, even though she was only ten years old. Mary, from down the street, a young colored girl who helped out sometimes, was not there. She was often very helpful and thoughtful toward Momma and the girls and often washed dishes and cleaned up the kitchen while Momma took care of the twin babies. Daddy worked seven days a week running the Gulf station on Calhoun and Meeting Streets, so he wasn't

home much. Sometimes he would give Momma a little cash to give Mary, who in addition to other things
would help wash the diapers in a tub in the yard with
a scrubboard and hang them out on a line to dry after
wringing water out of them.

I rummaged around the small icebox in the kitch-
en, which still had a little bit of the block of ice bought
from the ice cart that came down the street a few
days ago. I found some baloney and mayonnaise and
then located some white Claussen's bread on which I
slapped some of the fat-loaded mayonnaise and one
slice of baloney and headed outside to gulp it down.
On the way I grabbed a clean grape jelly jar which we
saved to use as a glass. Once outside in the small yard,
I filled the jar with water from a spigot.

Climbing the Tree

I didn't know where brother Billy was, so I decided to shimmy up the knotted thick rope hanging down from the large limb from the big tree which grew in our neighbor's yard but hung over ours. We had found the large rope on a dock near the river and dragged it home. The first time we ever climbed onto the top of this tree, we got to it by shimmying up a pipe on the back side of our house and onto the roof and then to a branch hanging close by. We tied knots in it every few feet so we could grip on them when climbing up into the thick wisteria vines at the very top of the tree, which were now loaded with purple, sweet flowers hanging in clumps like grapes, entwined among the highest limbs of the tree. We liked hiding quietly and unseen up there among the leaves and thick vines like little monkeys where no one could see us from the ground. We even jumped from branch to branch without fear of falling because the vines were so thick and strong.

As I lay quietly among the strong vines surrounded by the soft leaves and grape-like flowers with sweet scents and staring at the blue sky above, I heard Ms. Rensford come out her back door into her small, manicured backyard with its brick-lined walkways surrounded by an old brick wall. Billy and I had helped her lay out the brick-lined walks that were now surrounded with pretty flowers. She had moved into the small house next to ours from New York. She was an artist of some sort who liked to use colored chalk for her work. She even had Billy and me do long sittings while she drew a colored chalk picture of each of us. She must have felt sorry for us because she often left snacks for us on the wall next to our house, including some Collins mix in a half filled bottle.

As I dozed off among the vines and the singing birds, my thoughts wondered to my emergency visit earlier in the year to St. Francis Hospital about three in the morning. After I woke up to terrible stomach pains, Mom and Dad rushed me to the hospital. Once at the hospital I was rushed in on a wheelchair and right away to surgery in fear that my appendix was about to burst. I still remembered the nurses dressed like nuns with white caps. Once in the operating room they put a mask on my face and asked me to count backward from ten as they dripped ether onto the mask. I didn't feel anything after reaching seven. I remember floating up to the ceiling above the bright lights in the dark shadows where I looked down upon the scene. Maybe I was close to dying.

I stayed in the hospital for almost two weeks and had a huge bandage covering the long five-inch incision with at least seven stiches on my lower right abdomen. The best part of being in that condition was all the comic books I got to read. Adventure ones were the best, but *Tales of the Crypt* was my favorite. It was over a week after leaving the hospital before I went back to school.

OLD HIGH SCHOOL OF
CHARLESTON ON SOCIETY STREET

We were not sure what this old building was, but we worked our way up to the porch area behind the columns by squeezing through a locked gate on the left side facing the street. There was a front door that was also locked but not really tight. We were able to squeeze through it too and came into a large auditorium with wooden seats lined in tight rows facing a wooden stage. Nothing much was in there and it was dark, and we played hide and seek for a while and then headed back outside.

We found a door on the right side of the building with some things stored in it including some old, large paintings. We left the stuff alone and headed to the backyard behind the building where we found a large mound with an opening on top. Looking down into it, we weren't sure what it was but it looked like a little channel with water trickling through it. We climbed down into it and didn't see anything of much interest so we left it and looked around back some more. We saw a brick wall separating the yard from a house behind it. A garage type building was up against the wall with what looked like a storage area on the top of it.

Those Yankees Wondered about Boiled Peanuts

The next morning being a Saturday free of school was time to roam. Billy and I decided to head down to Mrs. Brown's peanut place that Momma introduced us to, to see if we could get some baskets of peanuts to sell along King Street. We found her in her backyard, a small place below and behind where she lived between Market and Broad Streets and in which she was boiling some peanuts in a large washtub over an open fire. The heat around it was pretty intense and caused her smooth, plump face to shine red and her blue eyes to stand out. She was always friendly toward us and gave each of us a basket with ten parched and ten boiled bags of peanuts. She told us to sell them for ten cents a bag and she would give us three cents for each one we sold.

Billy said he'd head to the Battery while I covered King Street between Broad and Calhoun and then Marion Square. As usual, I was barefooted so I stuck to the shady, cooler side of the street as I walked along hollering, "get your hot boiled peanuts now, only ten cents a bag!" Occasionally a northerner would stop and ask me what boiled peanuts were since they had never heard of them, sort of like them wondering what grits were. I could usually get a few of them to try a bag and show them how to eat them. Some just preferred the parched or "roasted" ones as they called them. Before reaching Marion Square, I'd sold about seven bags and headed toward the Old Citadel Military dormitory that looked sort of like a gray fortress where I knew I could go up the stairs located in each corner of the quadrangle. I enjoyed climbing up the stairs and walking around the old place, and I'd try to sell some nuts to people I saw coming or going from the offices, stressing the delight of the boiled ones.

That day I only sold two bags before heading back down the stairs and out the entrance from the quadrangle onto Marion Square. The day was warm and time had flown, so I headed back quickly along King

Street where I sold two more bags before reaching Mrs. Brown's where I returned my leftover bags, gave her my collected dollar and ten cents, and got thirty-three cents in return.

I had been to the Coast Guard station on the Ashley River near the end of the Battery before and thought about trying there again soon. The last time I was there, the sailors let me come on board one of the ships and sell my peanuts. They always bought a few bags. I could smell aromas of food cooking on the ships and cigarette smoke.

On the way to Mrs. Brown's, I peered briefly into the vented grates on the sidewalk, and I thought I spied a few coins down in the dirt along with cigarette butts and trash collected in the bottom. I could smell strange odors coming up from underneath the buildings next to these grates. I planned on looking closer into them later. I had an idea about how to reach those coins.

The sweetness of the scent grew stronger as we went.

As we crept closer, they spied us on the wall and wondered if we would fall.

We usually went to church on Sunday because of Momma. We normally wore dark blue pants and a white, short sleeved shirt that she had for us. Mine was always too small and my brother's too big, which I think were probably hand-me-downs from one or more of our older, upstate, Florence area cousins. This Sunday morning Momma wanted us to go to church, but we decided to skip Citadel Square Baptist because we didn't have any clean church clothes or decent shoes. Our old, brown, stinky leather shoes had soles worn through and we had stuffed cardboard inside them. We'd also wrapped black tape around the toe box because the soles had come loose from the upper leather part, so we preferred going barefoot. About this time, two doors down, colored people were beginning to gather at the old Episcopal church with the big red door and large side windows. Folks who lived nearby walked to the church in their Sunday best and some others came in cars and parked along the street.

We left the house and hurried, barefooted down the street to just past the church three doors up from home where the black folks worshipped and that needed some fixin' up. It was a big-fronted building with tall windows all around. The windows always seemed to be open so they could catch the breeze no matter what time of year. We could already hear the regular Sunday morning clapping, stomping, and singing that you could hear all the way to George Street up by the Catholic church on the corner.

As we got closer the aroma hit us. So much cologne and perfume was splashed on by the folks in church that whiffs of old lilacs and rose water drifted up the street to meet us as we passed Finkelstein's Royal Food Market on the corner of Anson and Laurens Street. After being exposed to these aromas several times, I always remembered the words from one of our many cousins, "smells like Sunday church" whenever he was around a bunch of ladies.

Right next to the church was a brick wall that started right on the edge of the sidewalk on Anson Street. It ran down along beside the churchyard and the parsonage behind it. I think it was put there by the people in the house next to it. That house was big and always seemed to be overgrown and empty. We just couldn't resist climbing up that wall this Sunday, after shucking our church clothes. We were like curious cats wanting to get a peek at what all that whooping and hollering was about coming out of those windows. We climbed down the wall and found a neat little perch on the roof of the outhouse turned bathroom next to the wall. We could see colored folks jumping, clapping, and arm waving in the air and the volume made your ears ring even though the church was only half filled. The preacher spied us on the roof through the window and his stern look got us to move quickly back onto the wall where we scampered carefully and swiftly further down toward Meeting Street, gripping the old worn brick with our bare feet. Not too fast, lest the preacher think that we weren't supposed to be there

and we would attract too much attention from others.
We acted like two little boys on a mission.

The Church and the Walls

THOSE LOVELY WALLS WERE THERE
TO DIVIDE THE YARDS THE HOMES HELD DEAR.
ATOP WHICH LITTLE BOYS SCAMPERED ALONG
PERHAPS IN PLACES THEY DID NOT BELONG.

This wall was an old one, made of brick with a narrow top, but our bare feet seemed to help us find the right steps to keep our balance. On we went to the end of that one section until it cut

sharply back to the right and we followed it, both crawling and balancing as we went, like two

cats out on a stroll, to another wall and then another and another. We spied several Japanese plum trees in some backyards and noted them for future reference. We also found a huge pecan tree, loaded with green nuts, which hung over a flat-roofed garage on the Meeting Street side.

Some black folks lived back there too, and they had a fire in the yard with a big black kettle over it. They were boiling clothes, it looked like, because they had no running hot water in the house. A lot of those old slave quarters didn't have running water inside, just a spigot in the yard for all their water use. You couldn't tell how many lived in them. Clotheslines hung with ragged shirts and pants almost dragging the ground from their wet weight. Smells of collard greens cooking always seemed to be around, maybe ham hocks too. I was glad we weren't eating there. We would just crawl on by with no one seeming to notice us even though we held our nose and made wrinkled faces at the smells. We ended up behind Central Drugstore on Meeting Street, one block west from Anson. This was the first of many of our wall-walking adventures.

Once we got to know all the walls around us and where they led, it was like our own personal footpaths through backyards that were hidden from the street side view. We never got a harsh word or complaints from those wall walks, well except maybe once we did, for getting our pockets loaded with Japanese plums from a tree too close to resist. Some lady shouted at us so we just ran. Old Charleston is a maze of these brick walls separating and hiding some beautiful yards. Even the graveyards had walls; they were especially fun because of the looks we would get from those passing by when they saw us on them. Especially on Church Street by John C. Calhoun's grave.

There were some alleys up by Ogletree's store, past Hasell Street, not quite to Pinckney Street, that had some long walls. Good training for us. There were houses built right up beside the walls, becoming sort of a ledge to the house next to it. With our backs to the wall we would sidestep down them with glee, never fearing a fall to the ground. It wasn't any further down than we were used to jumping anyway. Some were higher, but so what? It was our path, our place to play. Some of these alleys were used by hobos to drink cheap wine and just hang out in. There were lots of glass bottles, broken to cut bare feet. It never happened to us, nary a cut. Smelly, drunk hobos didn't chase us either.

We found canyons created by walls that you couldn't get to the top from the ground, limbs of trees ready to climb close at hand, and vines and flowers everywhere. We ventured out to other areas, some not on purpose or maybe so, and with a wondrous, "where does that go" curiosity as we just continued climbing up and following them wherever they went. We seemed immune from harm or "hey, what are you doing up there" calls. We never thought about whose yards or whose walls we were on. We were just two small boys, just curious, not up to mischief, escaping from our small, old home, in a run-down area, making the backyard walls our personal secret playground in the heart of a historic

old city. As time went on and after some serious training, conditioning, and experience, we even "graduated"
to some bigger things, perhaps a little too dangerous
for two young, free-spirited, adventure-seeking boys.

Hobos, Railcars, the Old Rice Mill, and Stinging Wasps

June had arrived and it was already getting pretty hot and humid in the afternoons in Charleston. Keeping the house windows open and the window fan on upstairs helped some but afternoon sweat was common. We stayed outside most of the time and often slept in the yard at night in some large, empty cardboard boxes we had dragged home from the appliance store on Meeting Street and stacked in our really small backyard.

Today we decided to head down Society Street across East Bay and past the J.T. Leonard vegetable distribution place near the railroad tracks where we would often see hobos (homeless boys?) sleeping in the bushes on top of cardboard. It could be a smelly place sometimes where dirty, poor-looking, glassy-eyed hobos with cheap wine bottles hung around. They had a spacey-eyed look, so we kept our distance. We played on some mounds of dirt and bricks and then looked inside one open railroad boxcar and saw a drunken hobo curled up in a corner, so we decided to stay out. We climbed up the ladders onto the top of a boxcar and scampered along the top between two connected cars. It felt good standing on top and seeing all around us like we were kings of the mountain! No one could see us from the ground up there, even when the train engine came along slowly to move some of the cars around to clear some track and we felt the jolt of the engine coupling onto our cars and start moving them. We figured we didn't want to ride far today, even though we had ridden them a ways before, even up as far as the Palace Theater on upper King Street, and so we scampered back down the side ladder as our car started moving really slowly and jumped to the ground and moved on.

BOX CAR HOBOS

Scrap Metal Hauls

I t had been a while since we came this way. Last time was to pull our Red Ryder, rusty, old wagonload of scrap metal, mostly iron pipes and similar stuff, to the junkyard near the end of Calhoun Street and close to the river. The old scruffy and dirty looking man, always smoking cigarettes, who worked in this trashy and dirty looking place, would sometimes weigh us on the large, heavy-duty scale with a large flat metal loading top he used for big stuff, not small stuff like ours. I think he was usually just being good to us little boys wanting a few pennies for our stuff we'd collected around the streets and empty lots.

Today we just continued along the winding trail that led through some high grass toward the old dark red brick building standing lonely between us and the river. We'd heard people call it the old rice building, but we didn't know why. Only the walls were now standing without a roof. We made it up over some crumbled brick mounds on one side and got inside. It looked pretty well traveled with packed dirt trails winding around mounds of stuff that had fallen from the roof, but there was no one in there today except us. As we scrambled along on a dirt path next to one wall, Billy suddenly screamed out horribly, "wasps!" He had bumped into a big nest on the side of the wall right near his head, and they were swarming out like crazy, all around his head, attacking and stinging him, causing him to scream in great pain. He ran like crazy toward home and I followed him as fast as I could. He had bumps all over his head and a few close to his eyes. Momma put cold water on his head and rubbed it with a paste she made out of baking soda, vinegar, and lemon juice, and that seemed to help. It took a while for the pain and swelling to go away but I sure felt sorry for him. This was something I hoped never happened again.

Why Do the Fish Croak?

Now that school was out for the summer, we had to find things to do outside because it was too hot and crowded inside. We'd noticed some little colored kids fishing at Colonial Lake and they were catching small fish that croaked like a frog; I guess that was why they called them croakers. We didn't have any regular poles so we found some small bush branches that were sturdy, and Momma gave us some thick sewing thread. We were lucky that Daddy had some spare small fishing hooks he gave us. For bait we decided to try some bread balls made from Sunbeam's white bread and that held together on a fishhook. As we headed down Society Street, I noticed one of my younger twin sisters following us. When we looked back, she would duck into a doorway thinking we wouldn't see her. We knew she wasn't supposed to be out and about by herself as she was too young, so we kept an eye on her. After a few minutes, I noticed she had sat down and was holding her foot and crying. So we ran back to check on her and found her foot bleeding from where she had stepped on some broken glass. We picked her up and carried her the few blocks back home, and Mom washed her foot off with a yard hose. It didn't look too bad and she stopped crying. Luckily Mom had a few Band-Aids and some Mercurochrome that she put on it.

The Coin Fishing Stick

If you look down, you may see,
A coin or two or maybe three.
Some coins, some bright, some dim,
I spied below the grate.
I wondered how they landed there, perhaps
from pockets of those who wait.
I made a tool to snatch them
from their place,
And they spread a smile upon my face.
And if you feel lucky and use some sticky gum
on the end of a stick,
You too can have some fun.

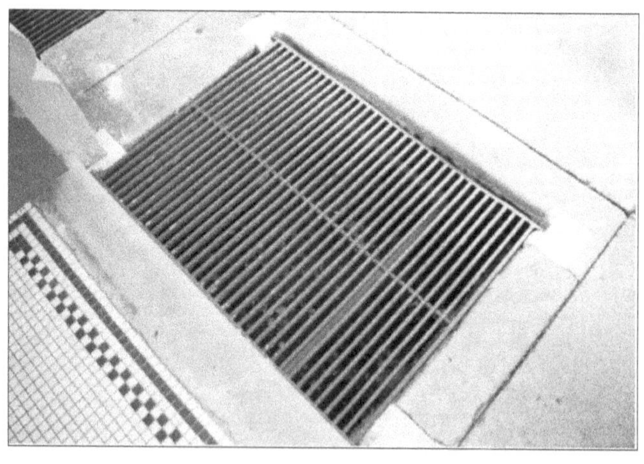

We decided to head back to Colonial Lake, but on the way I'd decided to try out something to get those coins we had seen below the grates on the sidewalks of King Street. I'd bought a pack of Juicy Fruit gum. Five gum sticks came in a pretty, yellow wrapping. The gum was stickier than most when you first started chewing it, so I figured it would work best for what I was about to do. As we came to a grate we knew had coins at the bottom, I pulled out a piece and chewed it until it was moist and sticky, then stuck it to the end of my branch I had brought along. I stuck it down through the grate and aimed toward a dime I had spotted. It worked! The dime stuck to the juicy gum, and I gently and slowly pulled it back up through the grate and grasped the dime before it fell off. I knew there were some pennies and nickels down there too, so I leaned down with my face almost touching the grate and spied them. After many attempts, making sure my Juicy Fruit was still stuck to the stick, I had recovered two nickels and six pennies. Along with the dime, that was twenty-six cents I had recovered. I felt rich and was already thinking I would be able to use my riches to go to the Palace Theater way up on King Street.

THE ANSONBOROUGH BOYS, STILL ALIVE BUT UP IN
AGE, CONTINUE TO SEEK ADVENTURES, EXPLORE NEW
THINGS, AND EXPAND THEIR MINDS.
PERHAPS YOU WILL SEE THEM HOVERING BY OR HEAR
THEIR SPIRITS IN THE WIND.
JUST LOOK AROUND AND YOU MAY SEE THEIR SIGNS,
AMONG THE YOUNG AT HEART AND THEIR KIN.
PEACE AND LOVE BE WITH YOU.

OLD SLAVE QUARTERS ON SOCIETY STREET

Quarters where enslaved people resided on
Society Street, photograph by George W. Johnson,
Charleston, South Carolina, ca. 1930, courtesy of
Gibbes Museum of Art.

PROPERTY FILE - 63 ANSON STREET
(SUSAN ROBINSON DEPENDENCIES)

Constructed ca. 1839; rehabilitated mid-1960s. One of two small gable-ended, masonry buildings (63 and 65 Anson Street) constructed as dependencies for 48 Society Street. Mrs. Robinson rented these properties separately before the Civil War. 63 Anson Street is listed as having been occupied by slaves in the 1861 census. Three files contain documentation of the covenant on the property; annual inspection reports; requests for alterations; documentation related to the covenant and to the sale of the property; documentation of the management of the property; house history (FOH, 1967); drawings (see mgmt. folder); copy of HCF covenant information card; documentation related to HCF's purchase

PROPERTY FILE - 67 ANSON STREET (ST. STEPHEN'S EPISCOPAL CHURCH)

Constructed 1835-1837. Built, and possibly designed, by John and Henry Horlbeck. The church's restrained classicism is evident in its arched center doorway, surmounted by a tablet and flanking stucco recesses with interspersed Tuscan pilasters on three sides of the building. The simplicity of the interior is relieved by the Doric columns supporting the gallery, the barrel-vaulted ceiling, and the arched chancel window. Also of interest are marble memorials to Sarah Hopton Russell and Sarah Russell Dehon. File contains narrative history; house history from Information for Charleston Tour Guides; photocopies of ARP photographs; measured drawing of interior floor plan; newspaper articles.

To be continued...

From my chair I stared upon a screen,
And began to wonder about a stream.
I spied a bird upon my windowsill
And wondered if I had lost my will,
To scamper upon the woodsy trails
Or dance among the hilly vales.
I resolved to leave my perch
And once again begin a search.

Old High School of Charleston on
Society Street